TEACH US TO PRAY

A LITTLE BOOK ON CHRISTIAN PRAYER

By The Most Rev. Dr. Charles Jason Gordon
Archbishop of Port of Spain

Sophronismos Press
Louisville, Kentucky

Copyright © 2019

†The Most Rev. Dr. Charles Jason Gordon
Archbishop of Port of Spain
All rights reserved.

No part of this book may be used or reproduced in any manner whatsoever without permission except in the case of brief quotations embodied in critical articles or reviews.

First Printing: November 2019

ISBN: 978-1-7335457-1-6

ADDRESS:
27 Maraval Rd
Maraval
Trinidad and Tobago
Caribbean

Email: abcjg@catholictt.org

CONTENTS

Introduction 11
1. Why Do We Pray? 15
2. Prayer – Covenant and Communion 21
3. God is Our Daddy! 27
4. We Should Be On Our Knees 35
5. God is Not a Slot Machine 43
6. "Do Not Abandon Us In Temptation" 49
7. Discernment of Spirits 55
8. The Rhythm and Routine of Prayer 61
On A Personal Note 69
Selected Bibliography 73

TEACH US TO PRAY

A LITTLE BOOK ON CHRISTIAN PRAYER

A Little Book on Christian Prayer

ACKNOWLEDGEMENTS

I would like to thank the many people who have encouraged me to write. Specifically, I'd like to mention Deborah de Rosia who encouraged me to write a series of teachings on one topic. The result is this little book.

I would like to thank also my proofreaders, Msgr. Cuthbert Alexander and Ms. Kathleen Maharaj, who laboured through the text several times to bring it to completion. Thanks also to Sr. Angela Ann Zukowski, MHSH, D.Min who did the reflection questions for each chapter. A deep debt of gratitude to Paula Persaud who designed the book and patiently made corrections and additions as was necessary.

Most of all, I'm grateful to Almighty God, Daddy, who continues to surprise and entice me with His incredible love, patience and care.

A Little Book on Christian Prayer

INTRODUCTION

Prayer for Christians is not an optional extra; it is the foundation of our life in Christ. It is what sustains daily life and helps us to grow into saints. Like water for the fish, air for mammals, and food for us humans, prayer is vital for life. Without it we die. There is no substitute – no workaround. Without a regular prayer routine we will be lured into all the distractions of our age and find that we may make great external progress, but feel empty and hollow on the inside.

Over the last years, listening to our young people, their catechists and parents, it is clear to me we are not giving them what is required for discipleship. Many young people, after a two-year Confirmation programme, come away with either no sense of prayer or a very undeveloped form of prayer. If our Church is to fulfil Christ's mandate to form disciples, then we need to teach every Christian to pray.

This little book, *Teach Us to Pray*, is my way of inviting the whole Church to this necessary practice of discipleship. Prayer is not, in the first instance, about techniques. It is about disposition and relationship. The technique will come if we have the right disposition towards God, and thus, the right relationship with God.

With the right disposition – a Christian disposition rooted in the Gospels – a conversation with God is an incredible prayer, as we come to know who we are in Christ Jesus our Lord. Moreover, we get to know our Father and His awesome love that is always present in little and great things. We recognise that God's love has been pursuing us long before we ever knew it. Prayer is about this love – from beginning to end. This disposition towards love and the relationship with a loving Daddy is what Christ taught his disciples. This I want to pass on to you.

The evangelist says: "God is love. Whoever lives in love lives in God, and God in them. This is how love is made complete among us so that we will have confidence on the day of judgment: In this world we are like Jesus" (1 Jn 4:16-17). Prayer is ultimately about learning how to receive, live and become love to others. Without this disposition and foundation, the technique will be interesting but it will not form us into the missionary disciples we are destined to become.

This book approaches prayer from different perspectives. Chapter 1 looks at why we pray. Chapter 2 looks at what prayer is. Chapters 3 to 6 delve into Jesus' teaching on prayer, seeking to uncover the elements of the disposition that Jesus taught his disciples. Chapter 7 looks at one of the great challenges for anybody who has become serious about prayer – understanding the inner and outer dynamics that cause frustration and bring temptations to quit. This is heavily indebted to St. Ignatius' Discernment of Spirits. Chapter 8 focuses on techniques and identifies some online tools that will assist you in creating a routine of prayer.

These chapters appeared previously as separate columns in the *Catholic News*, the weekly newspaper of the Archdiocese of Port of Spain, Trinidad and Tobago. By gathering them into this book on Christian prayer, it is my hope that these reflections will help you to dispose yourself to God more adequately. To do so is the first step in preparation to plumb the depths of God.

Charles Jason Gordon
Archbishop of Port of Spain
Easter Monday, 22 April 2019

A Little Book on Christian Prayer

CHAPTER ONE

WHY DO WE PRAY?

Prayer for the Christian is like water for fish. It is through prayer that we realise the full measure of God's intention for us – mystical union with the Trinity.

To pray is to realise the truth that we are in God. This is not the usual experience of our day or our life but it is the truth. We are in God in a very special way. Prayer does not bring this about. It allows us to realise this union and give way to God.

Pray Always

Writing to the Ephesians, St. Paul says in "all your prayer and entreaty" keep praying in the Spirit on every possible occasion. Never get tired of staying awake to pray for "all God's holy people" (Eph 6:18).

The text is important for several reasons. First, note the double *all*: all your prayer, and on every occasion pray for all God's people. St. Paul is leaving nothing to chance. This is as inclusive as possible. The Christian is called to pray constantly and the prayer should be in the Spirit, and offered for all the saints.

The fuller text, Eph 6:10–20, speaks about putting on the armour of Christ. St. Paul lists six items worn by the Roman soldier: belt, breastplate, shoes, shield, helmet and sword. Then comes our verse about prayer. The invocation to prayer is not the seventh item of clothing to be put on; it is the portal through which the other six make sense.

This call to pray constantly arises from St. Paul's understanding of the life of grace of the believer. Let us explore the Letter more deeply to follow his logic.

Overview

In his book *The Message of Ephesians*, John R W Stott divides the text into four sections:

1. The new life which God has given us in Christ (1:3–2:10).
2. The new society which God has created through Christ (2:11–3:21).
3. The new standards which God expects of His new society, in particular unity and purity (4:1–5:21).
4. The new relationships into which God has brought us –harmony in the home and hostility to the devil (5:21–6:24).

This flow of the text allows us to begin understanding the insistence on prayer. To understand better we need to look more deeply at a pivotal text in the Letter, Eph 2:3–10. It states:

> But God, being rich in mercy, through the great love with which he loved us, even when we were dead in our sins, brought us to life with Christ (it is through grace that you have been saved) and raised us up with him and gave us a place with him in heaven, in Christ Jesus. This was to show for all ages to come, through his goodness towards us in Christ Jesus, how extraordinarily rich he is in grace. Because it is by grace that you have been saved, through faith; not by anything of your own, but by a gift from God; not by anything that you have done, so that nobody can claim the credit. We are God's work of art, created in Christ Jesus for the good works which God has already designated to make up our way of life.

Prayer is a response to what God has done for us in Christ Jesus. It is by recognising the generosity of God to us that we are moved to be generous to God.

This movement is prayer: the giving of ourselves in love to a loving and merciful God. It is the only response that makes sense given the extraordinary nature of the grace that we have received. We pray because we have been loved incredibly by God.

The Mystery

Mystery is central to the inner logic of the text: We were (1) dead to sin, 2:5; (2) brought to life in Christ, 2:5; (3) saved by His grace through faith, 2:8; and (4) reconciled by God – Jews and Gentiles – to form one body, 3:9.

In Ephesians 3, St. Paul speaks about the mystery (v 3,4,6,9). He says: "This mystery is that through the gospel the Gentiles are heirs together with Israel, members together of one body, and sharers together in the promise in Christ Jesus."

At the core of the mystery is the constant phrase: we are "in Christ." Read Eph 1:3–14, the prayer at the beginning of the Epistle. St. Paul uses "in Christ" at least 11 times. We are in Christ as a fish is in water.

To pray is to recognise the truth that we live and move and have our being in Christ; to remain connected to the core of our spiritual life. It is to recognise that when we were dead in our sins, God raised us to life in Christ. This raising to life is the most precious gift we have ever received. Prayer is a response to the gift of grace that we have freely received from Christ.

To deepen our understanding, St. Paul uses the metaphor of the union of a married couple to speak about our participation in Christ – the total intimacy to which we are called.

This is the point and purpose of prayer: to understand the depth of the mystery from inside. We are alive in Christ and are called to nuptial union. It is through prayer that we discover the deepest truth of our being – we are children of God. So it is not God who needs our prayer. It is we who need prayer to remain alert to the truth of who we are in Christ.

> **Key Message**: Prayer is necessary for our sake; it allows us to live the full truth of our call from God by realising the intimacy to which we are called.
>
> **Action Step**: Review your prayer practice and commit to increasing your rhythm of prayer to a daily practice with a fixed way of praying – *Lectio Divina*, Mass, Eucharistic Adoration, Rosary, Prayer of the Church, the Examen prayer (See Chapter 8).
>
> **Scripture Passages**: Read the Letter to Ephesians; meditate especially on the two prayers – 1:3–14 & 3:14–21. Also, meditate on the key text where St. Paul shows us what we have received in Christ: Eph 2:3–10 and 3:3–9.

CHAPTER 1:
WHY DO WE PRAY?

1. What is my understanding of prayer or praying?

2. What role or place does prayer have in my daily life? Do I "say prayers" or "pray," or both? Explain.

3. How would I describe my prayer life?

4. Archbishop Gordon states: "We pray because we have been loved incredibly by God." How do I experience this love? Do I respond with gratitude?

5. The call to be missionary disciples is challenging in our modern world. What steps or actions have I embraced to stay focused on Jesus' invitation to me?

To watch a video on this topic, go to:
http://bit.ly/christianprayerchpt1

CHAPTER
TWO

PRAYER – COVENANT AND COMMUNION

Having looked at why we pray, now we will look at what prayer is. Remember from the perspective of the Letter to the Ephesians, prayer is necessary for the Christian to recognise the truth – we are in Christ like a fish in water.

This awareness is essential for the Christian to remain alive in Christ and grow to the full measure to which he or she is called. This growth in Christ is the essential element of discipleship.

This is not a metaphor: it is a reality – the goal and fulfilment of all human living. We have the capacity for a relationship with God. More than that, we have the capacity for union with God. As St. Augustine says so beautifully, "My soul is restless O Lord, till it rests in you."

I answer the question "What is prayer?" to help initiate you into the sacred mysteries of God, into the way of the heart, the life of grace. I hope you will begin to understand the spiritual life from a much bigger perspective, as not one life among others but rather a dimension of human living that, if explored and developed, opens all other dimensions to incredible fruitfulness.

About prayer, St. Thérèse of Lisieux says: "For me, prayer is a surge of the heart; it is a simple look turned toward heaven, it is a cry of recognition and of love, embracing both trial and joy" (*The Autobiography*).

This is a relationship description. It speaks to lovers and to desire; it is a matter of the heart, yet it is not attached to a particular outcome. It will receive either trial or joy; there is a holy indifference.

The *Catechism of the Catholic Church* (CCC) has a short section on the nature of prayer that can lead us in exploring this rich treasure.

Prayer as a Gift

The Catechism defines prayer as "the raising of one's mind and heart to God" (CCC 2559): not just the mind, but also the heart. We raise our thoughts and affectivity (feelings and emotions) to God.

What is the raising of the mind? It is the conscious act of shifting the mind from all that occupies it towards God who is its true subject. By this definition no other activity is necessary for prayer: no words, no action, no gestures are required.

It is not about saying prayers; it is about praying which begins with the raising of the mind and heart to God. This purity and simplicity is what prayer is really about. There are many ways to achieve this.

The second part of the same text says prayer is "the requesting of good things from God." This is a second disposition, one of petition, requesting grace and favour from God. This leads us to consider the type of relationship into which we are invited, and the assurance we should have before a wonderful Father.

The third part of the text addresses the kind of attitude or disposition. It asks, "But when we pray, do we speak from the height of our pride and will, or 'out of the depths' of a humble and contrite heart? He who humbles himself will be exalted; humility is the foundation of prayer. Only when we humbly acknowledge that 'we do not know how to pray as we ought,' are we ready to receive freely the gift of prayer. 'Man is a beggar before God.'"

Disposition of the heart is far more important than words or gestures. Humility is what opens the prayer to efficacy, because it opens the relationship with God to trust and depth.

To come to prayer with pride and arrogance is to close off the relationship before we begin. Remember, pride is the first of all sins (Gen 3), and the gateway to all the other deadly sins. Because prayer is relationship and love, pride and arrogance have no part in it. We need humility to pray, but it is only through prayer that we become truly humble. For, as the text says, prayer is a gift from God.

Prayer and the Covenant

Covenant is the way God chose to structure our relationship. A covenant is a binding agreement between two parties.

In the *Bible*, God made successive covenants with the Jewish people and the final covenant with the Blood of His Son Jesus Christ. Through each covenant God developed the relationship and steps and stages.

The covenant structures the relationship between God and us. Prayer builds that relationship and deepens it. Prayer is the heart of discipleship because it is what unites us to God in the new covenant (cf CCC 2564). He is the vine and we are the branches: Cut off from Him we can do nothing. It is through prayer that we abide in Him, or at least become conscious of abiding in Him.

Prayer as Communion

The text says: "In the New Covenant, prayer is the living relationship of the children of God with their Father who is good beyond measure, with his Son Jesus Christ and with the Holy Spirit. The grace of the Kingdom is the union of the entire holy and royal Trinity ... with the whole human spirit" (CCC 2565).

Prayer is a relationship: it is Trinitarian – about the union of God with the whole human spirit. This is central to any Christian understanding of prayer and the way we pray. God is not a slot machine who dispenses goodies as we play our chances. God is a Father who loves us and wants union with us here and now, and complete union in the next life. This union with God is at the heart and centre of all Christian prayer. It is in and through prayer that we experience ourselves as beloved of God. This identity as beloved son or daughter is essential to discipleship, to union with God and becoming our best selves.

As St. John Paul says in his Apostolic Exhortation *Familiaris Consortio*, On the Family, 62: "It should never be forgotten that prayer constitutes an essential part of Christian life, understood in its fullness and centrality. Indeed, prayer is an important part of our very humanity: it is 'the first expression of man's inner truth, the first condition for authentic freedom of spirit'."

> **Key Message**: Prayer is a relationship with God. It is Trinitarian. It is a covenant and communion.
>
> **Action Step**: Read the text on Christian prayer in the Catechism (CCC 2558–2565).
>
> **Scripture Passage**: Jn 15:1–17.

CHAPTER 2:
PRAYER: COVENANT AND COMMUNION

1. What does it mean for me to be "alive in Christ"?

2. The *Catechism of the Catholic Church* defines prayer as having three elements. What are they, and how do they relate to my understanding and experience of prayer?

3. Why is humility essential for an authentic prayer life?

4. What image of God do I bring into my prayer life? How does it relate to the ideas put forward by Archbishop Gordon?

To watch a video on this topic, go to:

http://bit.ly/christianprayerchpt2

CHAPTER THREE

GOD IS OUR DADDY!

HOW DO WE PRAY? – Part 1

Jesus' disciples asked the question – "Lord, teach us to pray, just as John taught his disciples" (Lk 11:1). At Confirmations I often ask those who have been confirmed about their prayer life.

Too often it is very undeveloped or their response awkward. Jesus' disciples had a similar problem. Prayer and discipleship are inseparable. John taught his disciples to pray but Jesus' disciples did not feel competent about their prayer. So they asked and Jesus taught.

What he taught is a treasure. It is a prayer; it is also our best insight into Jesus' understanding of God. It is a spirituality. The Fathers of the Church teach that this prayer is the norm or measure for all Christian prayer.

The Prayer

I will use the version we say at Mass.

(a) Our Father, who art in heaven,
hallowed be thy name;
(b) thy kingdom come,
thy will be done
on earth as it is in heaven.
(c) Give us this day our daily bread,
(d) and forgive us our trespasses,
as we forgive those who trespass against us;
(e) and lead us not into temptation, but deliver us
from evil.

This is a beautiful direct prayer addressed to God by someone with absolute trust and confidence. This is the first striking thing: it puts the person praying in a very specific disposition, one essential for all Christian prayer.

People divide the prayer in several ways. Without being too technical, I like to see it in two parts (a) and (b); (c) to (e). The first part gets the disposition right, the second asks for what we need. Both parts work together to form the perfect prayer.

Our Father

God is our Father. These first two words are in themselves a meditation. God is Father. Jesus calls God "Abba," a loving Father. This is a revolution in spiritual history – unprecedented. He does so in the Garden of Gethsemane, sweating blood and tears (Mk 14:36).

The term "Abba" is one of endearment, as when a child speaks to his daddy, entrusting himself into Daddy's arms – throwing caution to the wind and abandoning all self-respect and societal decency; calling God "Pops," "Daddy," "Ole Man," is a sign of a most familiar and affectionate relationship. Yes, the deepest truth about God that Jesus reveals is that God is your Father. God is both our Father and Jesus' Father.

The father is the first other with whom we come into contact. We are in Mum for nine months and then she feeds us and we are still connected to her. The baby sees Mum as an extension of self for many months.

Dad is the first other we encounter. If this other is secure and trustworthy, then we learn to trust others. If this other is not trustworthy or absent emotionally or physically, then trusting others is extremely difficult.

Yet Jesus calls God "Abba." In doing this he is inviting us all into a healing experience with the ultimate Other, who is trustworthy and secure and both emotionally and physically present.

God is the ground of our being. But God is Father. The first invitation is to a relationship of love, to see God not as the old man with the long beard and stick, waiting to hit us if we mess up, but rather as a loving Father. We are God's children and God wants the best for us in every area of our life. This is the foundation of Christian prayer. It is all about love.

Love is the key through which we must interpret all of scripture and all of our existence. If anyone acknowledges that Jesus is the Son of God, God lives in him or her and that person in God (1 Jn 4:15). And so we know and rely on the love God has for us.

As the evangelist says further: "God is love. Whoever lives in love lives in God, and God in him. This is how love is made complete among us so that we will have confidence on the day of judgment: In this world we are like Jesus" (1 Jn 4:16–17).

When Isaiah prayed, "Oh, that you would tear the heavens and come down ... come down to make your name known to your enemies" (64:1–2), he did not know what he was asking. When Moses asked God: What is your name? (Ex 3:13). Jesus answered the question – God's name is Daddy.

This is the revolution in Christianity: We are not placating an angry god, a whimsical god or a capricious god. We are going into the arms of a loving Father who is always happy to embrace His child. This is the Christian understanding of prayer. Prayer is about love.

Our Identity

There are two commandments: Love God, and love your neighbour as yourself (Lk 10:27). This is why God is our Father. Not just my daddy but our daddy too. The first word of the prayer creates a second disposition – we are brothers and sisters for we have one Father.

The whole prayer flows from this disposition. The petitions in the prayer for bread, forgiveness and protection flow from our trust in Daddy and our participation in the family of God.

This is why the Catholic tradition has a well-established social teaching. If we are brothers and sisters then social justice is an integral part of prayer and of Catholic spirituality. We must treat each other rightly, be fair in all of our dealings and take care of those on the margins of society.

We must protect the poor, the vulnerable, the prisoner, the migrant and refugee. They are our brothers and sisters. We must also protect the earth, our common family home.

To call God "Our Father" has significant implications for how we pray; how we pray has significant implications for how we live. We are members of the family of God.

As St. John says: "See what great love the Father has lavished on us, that we should be called children of God! And that is what we are!" (1 Jn 3:1)

To use the words "Our Father" is to be invited into the mystery of the Body of Christ with Christ as our head and God as Our Father. It is to be initiated into sacred mystery where we begin to understand our interconnectedness. Our identity is connected to everyone else, especially the most vulnerable.

I had hoped to do the whole "Our Father" in one chapter, but this has not been possible. Let us take our time learning how to pray. It is the most important foundation for discipleship and for achieving the aspiration of our Church – that we will all be missionary disciples.

Key message: God is Daddy! Not my daddy but our daddy! We all belong to each other and must care for each other and our common home, the Creation.

Action Step: Stay with the words "Our Father" or "Daddy." Ask God to open your mind and heart to receive the grace to call Him "Daddy" from all of you, the depth of your being. Ask Daddy for the grace to see others as brothers and sisters.

Scripture Passage: Mt 6:9–13.

CHAPTER 3:
GOD IS OUR DADDY

1. When I pray the "Our Father," how conscious am I of the words? Do I pray them intentionally?

2. Are there any fresh insights from Archbishop Gordon to help me understand the term "Father" in prayer?

3. How is there a Catholic Social Teaching dimension in the "Our Father"?

To watch a video on this topic, go to:

http://bit.ly/christianprayerchpt3

A Little Book on Christian Prayer

CHAPTER
FOUR

WE SHOULD BE ON OUR KNEES

HOW DO WE PRAY? – Part 2

God is Daddy! A loving Father! This as we have seen is the foundation of Christian prayer. If it is love, it is real. It is about relationship and is reciprocal in nature.

It means abandoning ourselves into the arms of a loving daddy who lovingly receives us. So prayer could never be a one-way street. It is not saying prayers – our activity; it is an act of loving – mutuality. This means we bring everything to prayer: the good, the bad and the ugly. This also means that God receives all. So let us bring all to God.

(a) Our Father,
    who art in heaven,
    hallowed be thy name;
(b) thy kingdom come,
    thy will be done
    on earth as it is in heaven.

In the first part of the "Our Father," (a) and (b) above, note the place of *heaven* in the first and fifth lines. Our daddy is in heaven. And yet, God is Daddy – intimate, loving, kind and caring. This is a paradox.

Daddy is in heaven – Other, spiritual, on a whole different level. The prayer evokes the truth: when we pray we communicate with heaven, our true home. It is a long distance call. But this God is with us and in us; He makes His home in us (local call). This too is a paradox.

Heaven

In a homily on the "Our Father," St. John Chrysostom writes, "When He says, '... in heaven,' He says this not to limit God to the heavens, but to withdraw from the earth the one who is in prayer, and to fix him in the high places and in the dwellings above" (St. John Chrysostom, *Homilies on St. Matthew*, XIX, 6).

The reference to heaven is not to stress distance but to invite us to touch and dwell in our true home, if only for a short while. This heaven is not a geographical place but a dimension of reality that we cannot see until we are born from above (Jn 3:3).

This stanza of the prayer says our Daddy is the one who created the heavens, the earth and all there is within. Jesus ensures we do not domesticate God but rather that God raises us to the "high places and the dwellings above."

We live in such a materialistic world that it is easy to reduce God to our level. Christian prayer begins by raising us to God's level so we can touch what is true and beautiful and noble.

Take a look at the Book of Revelation, chapters 4 and 5. It paints a picture of heaven: The throne of the one of great age, the four creatures (symbols of the evangelists) singing, "Holy, holy, holy is the Lord God Almighty, who was, and is and is to come."

This is awe and reverence and otherness and worship. Daddy is so other that we should be on our knees, not because he wants it, but because "our God is an awesome God." To touch the divine is both a deep attraction and at the same time a deep wound. Our ego cannot continue with its deception in the face of the really real – Daddy who is in heaven. We try to bring everything to our level; prayer takes us to heaven our true home.

Hallowed be thy name.

This is best translated – "May your name be made holy," set apart and consecrated, wholly other. Is the petition asking that God make His name known so people reverence it as holy here and now? Or is the petition about making Daddy's name holy in our lives by how we live as individuals and society?

Here we see the paradoxical nature of prayer. It is both God's action and our action. By praying, we invite God to reveal the truth: Daddy is holy, other! As children, we are called to be holy, other!

We are called to love unconditionally, working tirelessly for justice and peace, to befriend and defend the poor. Prayer is not divorced from action; it is primarily about becoming a child of God and then living like God's child.

Thy kingdom come, thy will be done on earth as it is in heaven.

Jesus always preached the Kingdom of God. It is another way of speaking of heaven. It is about perfect harmony or union with God, self, neighbour and Creation. It is that dimension of reality that we touch imperfectly on earth when we encounter the risen Christ, surrender all to God and are reconciled with Him, self, neighbour and Creation.

It is like moving from a 3D world to a 4D world: a new dimension opens up that changes the whole way we experience reality. For those with the dimension of faith, the world is still the same but everything is so different.

We see harmony where others see difference. We see God breaking into every human experience, whereas others see matter and atoms colliding. We see a plan unfolding with love as the logic and motor of history. Others see power, sex or money as the motor of history.

The Kingdom is here and now for everyone but not everyone has touched and experienced this dimension of reality. Yet, the whole world is pregnant with God who is breaking through our resistance through seduction, to love us into being fully alive.

God is a consummate lover. The Kingdom of God is about love. In the "Our Father" we pray that this unstoppable love breaks through all our human resistance, so we live in love and understand that we all live in God.

Love needs freedom: freedom to respond or reject – to accept the invitation of this consummate lover that is God. So we pray that God's will be done, that we surrender to the desire and purpose God has for us. With God, His will is the manifestation of His love, for God *is* Love.

God's will is done perfectly in heaven. For those who experience living in the dimension of the Resurrection, the unstoppable love of God (heaven), the surrender to God's will is the surrender to becoming the best version of themselves.

For those who live only on earth without touching heaven, God's will seems like a burden and an oppression to be resisted. This is the drama of human history. Here is the stuff of war and strife and human rebellion to God. We make ourselves smaller and lesser creatures when we resist and rebel against God.

> **Key Message**: Encounter with Daddy is the invitation; prayer as a loving relationship is the sacred portal; and actively doing God's will is the requirement of living in the new dimension (heaven). We give God what is most precious – our free will.
>
> **Action step**: Look at the areas in your life where you resist God or rebel against God. Have an open conversation with God about these.
>
> **Scripture Passage**: Jn 3:1–21; Rev Ch 4, 5.

CHAPTER 4:
WE SHOULD BE ON OUR KNEES

1. What is my understanding of heaven?

2. To touch the divine is both a deep attraction and at the same time a deep wound." What does this mean?

3. How does my understanding of the Kingdom of God influence how I pray and interact with the people and events God places in my life?

To watch a video on this topic, go to:

http://bit.ly/christianprayerchpt4

A Little Book on Christian Prayer

CHAPTER FIVE

GOD IS NOT A SLOT MACHINE

HOW DO WE PRAY? – Part 3

The "Our Father" is an ancient prayer. Originally spoken in Aramaic, it was written in Greek, translated into Latin and later into English. This is why we have so many variations in the text, in different versions of the *Bible*.

We have seen thus far that God is our Daddy, we are brothers and sisters and we have a common home – this earth – to care for. We have also seen that Daddy is in heaven, which is first experienced imperfectly as a dimension of living where we come to reconciliation with God, neighbour, the Creation and self – in perfect harmony – surrendering our will to God's will.

This is how we find our highest good and truest self. So we pray, "Bend my heart to your will, O God." This single act of bending to God's will is the stuff of spirituality and holiness; how we become the best version of ourselves.

The first part of the prayer contained a statement to God and two petitions also addressed to God: the "your" petitions. The second part of the prayer focuses on the "us" petitions – give us, forgive us, lead us, deliver us.

While the first part of the prayer focused on heaven and the truth of our reality as children of God, the second part focuses on our needs while on pilgrimage on earth.

(c) Give us this day our daily bread,
(d) and forgive us our trespasses,
    as we forgive those who trespass against us;

Give us this day our daily bread.

This should be so easy! A child, asking Daddy for bread! Not for self, for it is *our* bread. Daddy will not give to one child and not to the whole family. All members of the family are included in this petition.

Bread is basic food that a contemporary of Jesus needed for life. The petition holds two concepts: (1) the bread is daily and (2) we only ask for today's portion.

This is reminiscent of the Exodus where the people collected "bread from heaven," every day, for that day (cf Ex 16:4 ff). They were forbidden to collect tomorrow's bread, unless it was the sabbath. They had to learn that God would supply the bread every day including enough for the Sabbath. Very slowly their trust developed that God would deliver and give what was needed, not only today, but every day.

This trust is the hallmark of Christian spirituality. It is the disposition we need to move to the next stage of the relationship with Daddy and to abandon our will to His will – to trust completely.

This unconditional trust of Daddy and gratitude for the daily gift of bread is what challenged the Israelites. It is what challenges us. Will Daddy give us every day what we need for this day?

The Christian is called to live within a tight space. At one end, God will give us what we need every day. At the other, the gift will be needs not wants. God is not a slot machine.

The ancient text has some challenges. In the Greek there is a word not found anywhere else in Greek literature or in the *Bible – epiousia.* ἐπίουσία (substance).

The Fathers of the Church have spilled much ink on this. St. Jerome translates it to supersubstantial bread. This concept holds two realities: (1) the Exodus – Bread from heaven and (2) John 6 – Bread of life that is real food.

St. Augustine interpreted it on three levels: (1) the things we need to sustain this life, (2) the sacrament of the Body of Christ which we may daily receive, and (3) our spiritual food – Jesus.

This petition is pivotal as it connects our deepest need with a loving daddy who gives us each day supersubstantial bread.

Prayer teaches us that we can trust Daddy to provide on the three levels. We move now from infancy in our faith journey. We are on our way.

Forgive us our trespasses.

From bread to forgiveness, from heaven to earth: we are confronted with truth. All have sinned and fall short of the glory of God (Rom 3:23). We cannot eat the bread of life if we are in rebellion against God (sin). So we ask for forgiveness.

We cannot have God on our terms. We cannot forgive ourselves (cf Mk 2:7). We need God as a fish needs water, so we ask for forgiveness. If we come to consciousness at all, we know the countless ways we are in need of mercy.

The word "our" in this petition sees trespasses as communal. This petition is asking for forgiveness beyond our own self. It connects our receiving forgiveness with our giving forgiveness to others – "as we forgive those who trespass against us."

This is the hard truth. We cannot ask God for mercy if we are not willing to forgive others. Our un-forgiveness is a cancer in the Body of Christ. We cannot raise our minds and hearts to God if we are holding un-forgiveness on earth. There are many parables that speak to this (see Mt 18:21–35).

Forgiveness challenges us at the core of our being. But this is why we need God. We cannot forgive without God's grace. Christian prayer brings us to this place where we know we are in need of mercy, for we know ourselves as sinners. Prayer changes us at the core of our being and is the engine of reconciliation between us and God, neighbour, Creation and self.

This petition catapults us into an adult faith. We have to do what we can for reconciliation. After all, God is doing everything to reconcile us in Christ. We who have received such extraordinary grace respond with generosity towards those who are in debt to us. We are starting to resemble the Daddy. The prayer is transforming us in the depths and in secret places.

> **Key Message**: Supersubstantial (daily) bread and forgiveness are key elements of the spiritual life. As we receive Jesus as Bread we are transformed into Christ and are given forgiveness. Now we too are called to forgive.
>
> **Action Step**: Reflect on your relationship with God: Is God a loving Father that you trust to give you what you need every day? Have this conversation with God. Look at the countless ways that God has forgiven you. Make a list of those who you find it difficult to forgive. Ask God's grace to bend your heart to forgiveness.
>
> **Scripture Passages**: Mt 6:9–13; Jn 6:25–59; Mt 18:21–35.

CHAPTER 5:
GOD IS NOT A SLOT MACHINE

1. The "Our Father" consists of two primary parts. Identify the focus of each part. Do I gain new insight from now being conscious of these different parts during prayer?

2. St. Augustine offers three levels for our understanding of "Bread of Life." What are they? How do I experience these three levels in my prayer life?

3. Why is the call to mercy and reconciliation essential for faithfully living out the "Our Father?" How can I live out this call daily?

To watch a video on this topic, go to:

http://bit.ly/christianprayerchpt5

CHAPTER SIX

"DO NOT ABANDON US IN TEMPTATION"

HOW DO WE PRAY? – Part 4

The "Our Father" is a gym for spiritual development and growth in discipleship, stretching the one praying just a bit more towards the goal – abandonment to Daddy.

Look again at the movement in the text: (1) God is Daddy (2) Daddy is in heaven – we are connected to the power of Creation (3) Learning to trust enough to bend our heart to Daddy's will (4) Trusting Daddy to give us every day what we need – most of all Himself as bread (5) Learning to let go and forgive – understanding the truth of our reality – we are sinners (6) Wrestling with evil – the role of temptation in the spiritual life (7) Deliverance from evil.

Each petition opens the question of faith at a very different level. If we do not see God as Daddy, how could we bend our will to His? How could we lovingly and trustingly ask for bread? How do we dare to forgive others? If we cannot do these, how do we resist temptation and, ultimately, how do we resist evil?

The interconnectivity of the prayer and its developmental steps makes it a gold mine for spirituality.

(e) and lead us not into temptation,
    but deliver us from evil

Lead us not into temptation.

This line has been the subject of controversy for years. It paints a very different image of God, at odds with Daddy God. It is an ancient translation, which makes God into the tempter and we weaklings begging not to be subject to this temptation.

Pope Francis has gone on record saying that the wording of the prayer should change, that the translation does not work anymore. There are many contending formulae.

The Spanish and French currently pray: "Do not let us fall into temptation." This changes the dynamic; Daddy God is on our side protecting us from falling. The Italians pray: "Do not abandon us in temptation" (*America*, Dec 8, 2017).

Temptation

The Greek word *peirazo*, used by St. Matthew and St. Luke, is most often translated as "tested." But it is also used to mean "tempted." There is a big difference, however. St. James uses the same word with both meanings:

"Blessed is the man who endures trial, for when he has stood the test he will receive the crown of life which God has promised to those who love him. Let no one say when he is tempted, 'I am tempted by God;' for God cannot be tempted with evil and he himself tempts no one; but each person is tempted when he is lured and enticed by his own desire" (Jas 1:12–14).

There is a difference between being tested and tempted. God may test, but never tempt. "Gold and silver are tested by fire but the Lord tests the heart" (Prv 17:3). St. Matthew says: "Then Jesus was led up by the Spirit into the wilderness to be tempted by the devil" (Mt 4:1). The Holy Spirit leads Jesus into the wilderness to be tempted. But note it is the devil who tempts.

It is in temptation that we come to the centre and core of the mystery of salvation: Whom will you serve? Will it be God or your desire? Remember Adam and Eve's: "I will not serve." Pride always comes before the fall. Through temptation we grow to trust God; we grow as children of God; we grow in holiness. We learn to put God first, before our desires.

Temptations exist because we have free will. Each temptation is an opportunity to exercise our free will and choose for God; to use what is most precious, the only gift that is worth anything at all to God.

In our choosing God, we demonstrate the depth of our love. God does not tempt us: that is what Satan does. God graces us in temptation and invites us to choose love and to grow up to the utter fullness of Christ.

Do not go looking for temptations: that is why we pray, "Do not let us fall into temptation." And when we are being tempted, we pray: "Do not abandon us in temptation." Both of these aspirations are contained in "Lead us not into temptation" and "Deliver us from evil."

Deliverance from Evil

The modern person does two things with evil. We either give evil more power than it actually has or we grossly underestimate it by reducing it to psychology and projection. Both of these are heresies.

The first constructs the world as a competition of two great powers – God and Satan – equal and opposite. This is a lie. God is God and Satan is a liar. Satan is a creature like us and so cannot be equal to God. This is vital to understand. The only power Satan has is the power we give him.

The art of evil is deception and the first and major deception is to get the person and the culture to either misrepresent or underplay the truth. Do not spend time on Satan and his kingdom, rather seek first "his Kingdom and his righteousness, and all these things will be given to you as well" (Mt 6:33).

Our generation also underplays evil as if it is a projection of humans. Well, it may also be that. Evil is real. We need to learn how to recognise its work and how to avoid its traps, snares and trials. We must reject evil. Key is that we cannot fight evil; nor do we have to. Jesus has already done that for us.

Through His unconditional love, by His absolute "yes" to God – even to death on the cross – Jesus defeated Satan. He put His life in the hands of God and trusted when trust did not make sense. In this act, evil was undone. Through freely choosing God's way we too undo evil.

Not only is Satan a liar, he is an idiot. His work of temptation can actually be the driving force to our holiness and growth in the spiritual life. Pray for deliverance from evil. This requires us to recognise evil, trust God and make the right choices.

> **Key Message**: Temptation is part of the spiritual life; we overcome it by abandoning ourselves to Daddy and accepting grace. This too is prayer.
>
> **Action step**: Look at the temptations you experience. Ask Daddy to spare you from these temptations and not to abandon you when in temptation.
>
> **Scripture Passage**: Mt 4:1–11

CHAPTER 6:
DO NOT ABANDON US IN TEMPTATION

1. Why is there controversy over the phrase: "Lead us not into temptation"? What is my view about it? How may it impact on how I pray the "Our Father"?

2. What is the difference between being tested and being tempted? How have I experienced both, and how did I respond?

3. What are the two heresies on the presence of evil in our world today?

4. How has my understanding or experience of evil changed during my lifetime? Has the change influenced how I pray?

5. What are the greatest challenges we face in the world today regarding belief in the presence of evil and Satan?

To watch a video on this topic, go to:

http://bit.ly/christianprayerchpt6

CHAPTER SEVEN

DISCERNMENT OF SPIRITS

WHY IS IT SO HARD TO BE CONSISTENT IN PRAYER?

If a profound and deep prayer life is so advantageous, why do so few people embrace the life of grace consistently? The answer is not an easy or straightforward one.

In his *Spiritual Exercises*, St. Ignatius gives us *14 Rules for Discernment of Spirits.* He begins by dividing humanity in two categories: (1) "Those who are moving from mortal sin to mortal sin" (Rule 1) and (2) "those who are making progress in their journey towards God" (Rules 2–14). It is important that at every stage we do three things – become aware, understand and then act decisively.

The "enemy of human nature" will encourage the person who is moving from mortal sin to mortal sin, who has been trapped by the appetites and living for pleasure, honour, power and wealth, to partake of all of the sensual delights, making these appealing.

In these persons, "the good spirit uses the opposite method, pricking them and biting their conscience through a process of reason." If the glory of God is man and woman fully alive (St. Irenaeus), then the opposite is man and woman fully dead. This is why Ignatius calls the evil spirits the enemy of human nature.

As we saw in the "Our Father," using our free will to choose for God is our most precious gift, the only thing that God will not take from us. Love requires free will; love requires choice. God will not take us against our free will.

The enemy of human nature is not a gentleman and will take us any way he can: enticement, deception, lies, addiction, etc. This is why Jesus counsels his disciples in the Garden: "Stay awake and pray not to be put to the test. The spirit is willing enough, but human nature is weak" (Mt 26:41). For the Desert Fathers, staying awake is the essence of spirituality – being aware, having understanding, and taking decisive action.

For those moving towards God, the roles reverse. Now, it is "the way of the enemy of human nature to bite, sadden and put obstacles, disquieting with false reasons, that one may not go on; and it is proper to the good spirit to give courage and strength, consolations, tears, inspirations and quiet, easing, and putting away all obstacles, that one may go on in well doing" (Rule 2).

It is God's intention to give us every grace to hasten towards the mystical union that Jesus promised us so the Father and the Son will make their home in us (Jn 14:23).

Consolation and Desolation

For a proper understanding of the 14 Rules and if we are to become aware of the stirrings of the soul, it is important to understand consolation and desolation, to become aware of which of these is dominant in our prayer at a specific time, and then what to do about it.

Ignatius says: "I call consolation every increase of hope, faith and charity, and all interior joy which calls and attracts to heavenly things and to the salvation of one's soul, quieting it and giving it peace in its Creator and Lord" (Rule 3).

Likewise: "I call desolation all the contrary of consolation, such as darkness of soul, disturbance in it, movement to things low and earthly, the unquiet of different agitations and temptations, moving to want of confidence, without hope, without love, when one finds oneself all lazy, tepid, sad, and as if separated from his Creator and Lord. ... As consolation is contrary to desolation, in the same way the thoughts which come from consolation are contrary to the thoughts which come from desolation" (Rule 4).

In our prayer as in our life, it is important to become aware when we are in either state. Do not worry about it; just notice it.

If in consolation, press on and enjoy the prayer and period of the journey. If in desolation, then there are some things that we need to know.

First, do not change the rhythm of your prayer or what you have previously offered to God. Second, it is to your advantage in desolation to extend your time of prayer and increase your devotion. Third, you must know and believe that this stage of desolation has its purpose and will come to an end. Take courage and resist despair, expecting to reconnect to God in your prayer and in your life.

When in desolation it is important to "make much examination of conscience" to see if you have slipped into sin, presumption, or pride. If none of these are true then stay the course, it is a time of purification. God is allowing this to wean you off the consolations of God and draw you to the God of Consolation.

This just means you are growing up. Smile, keep your chin up and keep pressing on. Do not despair; do not lose heart. This is a very fruitful part of the journey, which will show in a deeper commitment to God and your knowledge that it is God's grace that brings you through every stage.

The Enemy of Human Nature

Ignatius describes the enemy of human nature as "a petulant child." If you give into its demands, the tirade will overpower you. If you stand firm in faith and confidence in God, it will cower and submit. If you are going through a time of great inner upheaval, it is important to seek spiritual counsel from a spiritual director. The enemy loves secrecy and revels in keeping you isolated. Speaking to a trusted spiritual director will change the game significantly. Ignatius also describes the enemy as "a chief bent on conquering and robbing what he desires."

This is spiritual warfare; you are no match for the enemy of human nature. We need to bend our hearts to God's grace to overcome the attacks. If you were in his position, how would you attack you – What is your weakest point of defence?

When you answer this question, again become aware, understand and take decisive action to strengthen yourself at this point of attack, which for some will be anger or greed for material things (avarice). For others it may be overeating (gluttony) or lust, envy or unforgiveness, or not keeping your commitments to prayer and the spiritual life (sloth).

Pride is the gateway to all the deadly sins. It is always the hardest to detect. This is why regular Confession is vital for the spiritual journey. The more we can name our areas of weakness in humility and tears before God and the priest, the less vulnerable we become.

Remember the enemy of human nature is a deceiver and a coward who cannot stand up to the grace that God constantly gives. Give in to God then; resist the devil, and he will run away from you. The nearer you go to God, the nearer God will come to you (Jas 4:7–8).

> **Key Message**: It is not only flesh and blood against which we fight but against the rulers, authorities and powers of the dark world (Eph 6:12).
>
> **Action Step**: Become aware, understand and act decisively in your movement towards God. Read Ignatius' *14 Rules for Discernment of Spirits*.
>
> **Scripture Passage**: Jas 4:1–17

CHAPTER 7: DISCERNMENT OF SPIRIT

1. What are the obstacles and opportunities I encounter when striving to use my free will to choose for God? How do I respond to these?

2. The essence of spirituality is "being aware, having understanding, and taking decisive action." How will I go about making this a reality in my life?

3. What is the meaning of consolation and desolation in one's prayer life? How have I experienced either one?

4. What are the three things I need to do/know in moments of desolation? How can I ensure I act appropriately?

To watch a video on this topic, go to:

http://bit.ly/christianprayerchpt7

CHAPTER EIGHT

THE RHYTHM AND ROUTINE OF PRAYER

TEACH US WAYS OF PRAYING

To pray is to live and become fully alive in Christ. I will focus here on methods and tools to assist your prayer but, remember, proper disposition and desire are essential.

Prayer is raising the mind and heart to God. It is a conversation with God and sitting in His presence. Prayer is a cry from the heart to a loving Daddy. You will be drawn to one type of prayer more than others. The best prayer is the one we make a habit of: we need a habit of prayer and a routine within the habit.

Daily Mass

Daily Mass creates a rhythm that sustains you. If you cannot participate every day, add at least one day to your weekend commitment. In the morning when you awake, read at least one of the readings of the day – either the Gospel or First Reading. Mull over it during the day.

At Mass, recognise that all gathered make up the Body of Christ and are integrally connected. Enter into an Examination of Conscience so as to identify your shortcomings. Ask God for mercy. Listen intently to the readings and homily for the word or phrase that God is speaking to you.

Offer yourself to God again in the Offertory. Pray through the Eucharistic Prayer, conscious of the One who comes to you on the altar. Receive Communion with full, active, conscious participation. Ponder the mystery of God becoming food for the journey.

Experience the sending off at the end of Mass as "missioning" you to go out into the world filled with Christ, to take Him wherever you go. But also, look for Christ in every situation.

Adoration

Go to Mass a bit earlier or sit in silence afterwards before the Blessed Sacrament, or visit one of the Blessed Sacrament chapels on a regular basis. Be conscious of the One before whom you sit. You can include other forms of prayer in this devotion.

Lectio Divina

For *Lectio Divina*, "Divine Reading," find a place conducive to prayer. Choose a scripture reading – the day's Gospel or First Reading and follow these steps:

- *Lectio*: Read the text slowly and prayerfully. The text is a portal through which we encounter the Living Word, Jesus Christ. We open our heart to the "tug"; listen for the word or phrase that captures our attention.

- *Meditatio*: Meditate on the word or phrase, mull over it, and begin a conversation with God as you delve deeper into the Word and the text. Is there a story in your life that is similar to the story in the text? What word is God speaking to you?

- *Oratio*: Respond to God from your heart; see what the text asks of you and respond, giving your "yes" to God. Are you ready to bend your heart to His will? Pray for the grace.

- *Contemplatio*: Sit quietly in a disposition of reception. Just be with God for no purpose or reason. Enjoy sitting in Daddy's presence. Experience the love.

Christian Meditation

The third-century Desert Fathers were champions at prayer, devoting their whole life to ascetical and spiritual practices. Their teaching is reflected in Christian Meditation, a prayer style developed by Abbot John Cassian (360–435). It comprises three elements:

- Posture: Sit in a chair with your back upright and feet on the ground. Hands on the knees either up for receiving or down for letting go. Become conscious of being in God's presence.

- Breath: Notice your breathing and then slow it down till the breath is slow, deep and rhythmic. Breathe from the belly. Let the breathing be deep, slow and constant.

- The word: Christian Meditation uses the sacred word *Maranatha* – "Come Lord Jesus." St. Paul uses the word at the end of his first letter to the Corinthians (1 Cor 16:22). It is also found in Revelation 22:20. It is an invocation, a cry from the heart, a plea to God to come to His children and not delay.

The word is said with every breath in four syllables – Ma-ra-na-tha. Some say the whole word while breathing in and again while breathing out. I split the word using two syllables on each part of the breath. This allows me to slow the breath even more.

The practice is 20 minutes in the morning and in the evening. But start where you are comfortable and build up to the 20 minutes. For more information visit the World Community for Christian Meditation (WCCM) website, wccm.org.

The Examen of Consciousness

St. Ignatius says if you do not have time, pray the Examen every day and you will not be far from God. The

Examen is a prayer process that invites you to reflect upon your day from five different perspectives. It is a recollection of the whole day, reliving the events and emotions.

- Become aware of God's presence. Recollect. Breathe, focus, and become aware.
- Gratitude: Reflecting on the whole day, to whom and for what are you grateful? Be grateful!
- Petition: Recollect the whole day again; consider your emotions during the day. Ask God to show you what He wants to teach you.
- Discern: Review the day again, discerning when you were the best version of yourself and when you were not. Ask the Holy Spirit to help you understand what led to the movements so you could learn from them.
- Forgiveness: Review the day again asking forgiveness of your Daddy for the times when you were not the best version of yourself. Imagine yourself in God's loving arms. Ask for mercy and experience it.
- Resolution: Prayerfully, resolve to move closer to being the best version of yourself.
- Conclusion: Pray for your loved ones and situations you will face tomorrow; enjoy the time with God and transition slowly out of the prayer.

Rosary

Saints were formed by praying the rosary. It is a prayer of giants. The mind meditates on the mystery being pondered, the lips say the words, the fingers slip each bead as you pray. Mary formed Jesus to grow in wisdom, stature and grace as a human; Jesus entrusted his beloved into her arms. She will form you and lead you to her Son.

Key Message: Prayer is possible anywhere, but we need to have a rhythm of prayer and a way of praying within the rhythm.

Action Steps: Choose from these prayers to anchor your morning and evening. Use one in the morning when you wake. Choose a second one for the evening. Both times need rituals of prayer. Pray the Examen. Download apps for Mass (Universalis) and Christian Meditation (wccm.org).

Scripture Passage: Lk 18:10–14.

CHAPTER 8:
THE RHYTHM AND ROUTINE OF PRAYER

1. Mass, Adoration, *Lectio Divina*, Christian Meditation, Examen of Consciousness and the rosary are forms and expressions of prayer that enhance our communion with God and one another. Identify the ones in which I currently participate. How can I deepen these practices, and further enrich my prayer life?

2. How can I share my experience with others?

To watch a video on this topic, go to:

http://bit.ly/christianprayerchpt8

A Little Book on Christian Prayer

ON A PERSONAL NOTE

This book is as much for me as for you. My reflecting on the various dimensions of prayer has renewed my commitment to pray. I hope and trust it has done the same for you.

I have known many times and seasons in my journey: times when prayer was absolutely exciting and compelling and other times when prayer was as dry as could be. Sometimes it seemed there was absolutely no response from God, regardless of technique. At other times the prayer blew me away by the depth of encounter and the overwhelming experience of God's love.

I have come to learn over the years that the depth of encounter may not always be a good indication of the quality of the prayer, for my dry and arid times have borne much fruit, even as the deep encounter has drawn me closer to Him. Every season in your life and in the life of grace is a good season, providing you are submitting your will to God's will. This is the ultimate test of prayer: are you becoming a better version of yourself? Are you surrendering to God?

It is the Father's desire to fill you to the utter fullness of Christ. What stops God? Your free will! You must want this grace. That is what prayer is, learning to want God above everything and everyone else; learning that our desire is so small in comparison to the desire God has for us.

Remember, God has asked us to pray always and at all times. This means that our whole life must become a prayer. This is not about technique; it is about recognising that God's promise is true.

> As the Father has loved me, so have I loved you. Now remain in my love. If you keep my commands, you will remain in my love, just as I have kept my Father's commands and remain in his love. I have told you this so that my joy may be in you and that your joy may be complete. My command is this: Love each other as I have loved you. Greater love has no one than this: to lay down one's life for one's friends. You are my friends if you do what I command. I no longer call you servants, because a servant does not know his master's business. Instead, I have called you friends, for everything that I learned from my Father I have made known to you. You did not choose me, but I chose you and appointed you so that you might go and bear fruit – fruit that will last – and so that whatever you ask in my name the Father will give you. This is my command: Love each other.

Jn 15:9-17

***May God bless you
on your journey to
mystical union with Christ.***

ON A PERSONAL NOTE

1. Periods of "dryness" in one's prayer life are not unusual. Have I experienced these? Was I able to remain focused on God's unconditional love for me?

2. What new insights have I gleaned from "Teach Us How to Pray"? How do I plan to integrate these into my life?

3. If it is true that "we live the way we pray and pray the way we live," has reading and reflecting on this book enabled me to see the relationship between my life of prayer and daily living (i.e. the Catholic Social Teachings)? Explain.

A Little Book on Christian Prayer

SELECTED BIBLIOGRAPHY

Catechism of the Catholic Church, 2nd ed. New York: Doubleday, 1995.

John Paul II, *Familiaris Consortio: The Role of the Christian Family in the Modern World*. Accessed January 5, 2019. Vatican.va.

Stott, John, R W. *The Message of Ephesians. Bible Speaks Today*. Illinois: InterVarsity Press, 1984.

Thérèse of Lisieux, *Story of a Soul: The Autobiography*. Translated from the original manuscripts by John Clarke OCD. 3rd ed. Washington DC: ICS Publications, 1996.

Made in United States
Orlando, FL
23 May 2024